MW00573187

PowerPhonics™

A Train on the Track

Learning the TR Sound

Sarah Sheffield

The Rosen Publishing Group's

PowerKids Press™
New York

A train runs on a track.

A train can be fast.

A train can carry people.

A train can carry trucks.

A train can travel above a road.

A train can travel above a river.

A train can travel under the ground.

A train can take you to work.

A train can take you on a long trip.

Would you like to try taking a trip on a train?

Word List

track

train

travel

trip

trucks

try

Instructional Guide

One of the essential skills that enable a young child to read is the ability to associate letter-sound symbols and blend these sounds to form words. Phonics instruction can teach children a system that will help them decode unfamiliar words and, in turn, enhance their word-recognition skills. We offer a phonics-based series of books that are easy to read and understand. Each book pairs words and pictures that reinforce specific phonetic sounds in a logical sequence. Topics are based on curriculum goals appropriate for early readers in the areas of science, social studies, and health.

Letters/Sound: **tr** – Write the words *tip* and *rip*. Remind the child that two consonants can be put together to make a new sound. Write the word *trip* and have the child decode it. Continue with *tack – rack – track*.
- Pronounce the following words, having the child write **t**, **r**, or **tr** according to the beginning sound: *truck, rat, train, town, trade, take, red, tree*. List **tr** words and have the child underline the **tr** in each one.

Phonics Activities: On a low bulletin board, display a construction paper engine and ten cars, five made from full sheets of construction paper, the other five made from half sheets. Fold both full sheets and half sheets lengthwise to form pockets. Assign a long vowel sound to each long car. Name words beginning with **tr** and write them on flash cards. Have the child place them in the appropriate train car. Short vowel sounds can be assigned to each short car and completed as a separate activity at a later time or as an ongoing activity. (Suggested long vowel words: *trade, train, tray, tree, treat, tried, troll, true, truth*. Short vowel words: *track, tractor, trap, trick, trip, trot, truck*.)
- Provide pictures of objects that start with **tr**. (Suggestions: *tree, truck, tray, train, track, tractor*.) Include a few other pictures that do not start with **tr**. Prepare cards with the names for each picture. Ask the child to match the words with the pictures. Have them pick out the picture-words that do not belong because they start with a different sound.
- Have the child complete open-ended sentences by choosing the appropriate **tr** word that makes sense in the sentence. (Examples: *Mary likes to [travel, take, tape] by [bus, train, car]. Bob and Tom [talk, trade, tell] baseball cards. The [truck, table, turtle] will drive to places in other towns.*)

Additional Resources:
- Barish, Wendy, and Gallimard Jeunesse. *Trains*. New York: Scholastic, Inc., 1998.
- Neye, Emily. *My First Train Trip*. New York: The Putnam Publishing Group, 1999.

Published in 2002 by The Rosen Publishing Group, Inc.
29 East 21st Street, New York, NY 10010

Book Design: Ron A. Churley

Photo Credits: Cover © Truitt Photographics/Index Stock; p. 3 © John Coletti/Index Stock; pp. 5, 7 © Telegraph Colour Library/FPG International; p 9 © Walter Geiersperger/Index Stock; p. 11 © Corbis; pp. 13, 15 © SuperStock; p. 17 © Bud Freund/Index Stock; p. 19 © VCG/FPG International; p. 21 © Amy Wiley/Index Stock.

Sheffield, Sarah, 1971-
   A train on the track : learning the TR sound / Sarah Sheffield.
      p. cm. — (Power phonics/phonics for the real world)
   ISBN 0-8239-5937-6 (library binding)
   ISBN 0-8239-8282-3 (pbk.)
   6-pack ISBN 0-8239-9250-0
   1. Railroads—Trains—Juvenile literature. 2. English language—
   Consonants—Juvenile literature. [1. Railroads—Trains. 2. English
   language—Consonants.] I. Title. II. Series.
      2001
   625.1—dc21

Manufactured in the United States of America